Ignite Your Potential

BREAK FREE FROM THE ORDINARY

GEORGE HATCHER

CasaHatcherPress

Introduction

Let's be clear from the very beginning: this is not a book written by a motivational expert. You will not find bullet-pointed lists of life hacks, nor will you hear from a guru standing on a mountaintop, dispensing universal truths. I am not an authority on how you should live your life. Far from it. For a significant portion of my own journey, I was an authority on how *not* to live, a case study in the destructive power of ambition when it's untethered from wisdom and foresight. What I do know, what I have earned through decades of trial and error—and some spectacular, life-altering failures—is the nature of my own self-motivation. It has been the engine of my life, a constant fire that has, at different times, either burned my world to the ground or illuminated a path toward a stable, meaningful existence.

This book is a tale of two lives, both lived by the same man. The first half was a storm. It was driven by a relentless, almost primal urge to achieve, to have, to conquer. When I was a young man, if I wanted something, my mindset was simple: "I'm going to have this, no matter what." That single-mindedness propelled me forward, allowing me to build businesses from scratch and expand them with breathtaking speed. But the "no matter what" came with a hidden clause, a price I didn't fully comprehend until the bill came due. I paid for that recklessness dearly. Without capital, I fueled my expansion with bad checks, building a sprawling enterprise on a foundation of fraud. Was it because my brain was fried from the sheer amount of alcohol I was consuming in those days? I can't say for sure, but the decisions I made were not those of a sound mind. That path didn't lead to lasting glory; it led, as it inevitably must, to a jail cell.

The stories in my earlier books, the *Pages of Passion* series, detail that chaotic first life. It was a life of chasing, of running, of flying too close to the sun and crashing back to earth. What you are holding now is an exploration of what came after the crash. It's about the second half of my life—a period now spanning more than thirty-eight years—where the fire of motivation didn't die out, but was instead channeled. The bumps in the road never disappear entirely, because life itself can be bumpy, but the self-inflicted chaos vanished.

In this second life, I reinvented myself. The same drive that had once pushed me into illegal schemes was redirected. I found a new calling, one that came looking for me: I became a trusted advisor to lawyers, a specialist in the delicate arts of client development and management. I discovered a "magic" in building relationships and managing expectations, guiding legal cases for clients across the country from afar. I still built businesses along the way, but they were different. They were built on solid ground, with thought, integrity, and patience—virtues I had little time for in my youth. I certainly didn't write any bad checks to get them started.

This book, then, is not the complete story of my life. That ongoing, raw, and detailed narrative can be found in my *Pages of Passion* series. Think of *this* book as something different: my own humble motivational guide, born from the wreckage and reconstruction of a life lived at extremes. The principles laid out in these pages—from shifting your mindset to building resilience and aligning your actions with your values—are the very lessons I learned through decades of struggle and reinvention. I don't want you to make the same mistakes I did. My hope is that by sharing my story first, you might gain some perspective on your own journey, on your own fire, and on the critical importance of deciding not just *what* you want to build, but *how* you choose to build it.

Dedication

Molly,

In the dance of life, you are my steady partner,

and in every melody, you are my cherished harmony.

With enduring love,

George

This book can be purchased at over 40,000 bookstores and libraries including brick and mortar stores, online, in print and digital, including Apple, Kindle, and Audible formats. Casa Hatcher Press is a subsidiary of Pretty Face, Inc. Rancho Mirage, California 92270.

Casa Hatcher Press. http://casahatcherpress.com (800) 416-6189

Book and cover designed by Casa Hatcher Press

Ignite Your Potential: Break Free From The Ordinary, by George J. Hatcher

First Edition July 2025

ISBN: 979-8-9989967-1-9 (Paperback)

ISBN: 979-8-9989967-2-6 (eBook)

Also By George Hatcher

Mario 1: Woman in Jeopardy

Mario 2: Coming of Age

Mario 3: Risky Business

Mario 4: Free Fall

Mario 5: Afire

Mario 6: Marked

Mario 7: Aftershock

Mario 8: Captivated

Single Titles

One Wilshire

Gabi

Rico

Cats: Meow Is The Language Of Love

HER: Artistic Expressions Through AI

Elegance In White: Through Wedding Gowns

Quinceañera Fashion: Fifteen & Fabulous

Billion Dollar Rainmaker Part I

Pages of Passion Book 1: My First 19 Years

Pages of Passion Book 2: Bold Beginnings

Pages of Passion Book 3: Rising Waves

Pages of Passion Book 4: Threads Of Destiny

Beyond The Scale: Health Benefits of Keto for Wellness

Cool Under Pressure: Warm With Humor

Love Is What It Is: Lessons From Everyday Life

Living Fully While We Wait to Die: Mindfulness Amid Mortality

Ignite Your Potential: Break Free From The Ordinary

Coming Soon

Chapter 1: Awakening the Fire Within

Discovering Your Why

Finding your purpose is a transformative journey that can breathe new life into your daily routine. Many people feel stuck in their lives, going through the motions without a clear sense of direction. This feeling of stagnation can lead to boredom and dissatisfaction. However, discovering your "why" can ignite a spark that propels you toward a more meaningful existence.

To uncover your "why," start by reflecting on your passions and interests. What activities make you lose track of time? What topics ignite your curiosity? These questions can help you identify what truly resonates with you. By focusing on what you love, you can begin to align your actions with your values and desires, creating a pathway toward a more fulfilling life.

Additionally, consider the impact you want to have on the world around you. Think about the legacy you wish to leave behind. Understanding how you want to contribute can provide clarity and motivation. When your actions are guided by a deeper purpose, even mundane tasks can feel significant, transforming your day-to-day activities into stepping stones toward your greater goals.

It's important to be patient and open during this exploration process. Discovering your "why" is not an overnight achievement; it requires introspection and experimentation. Allow yourself to try new things, meet different people, and explore various interests. Each experience will bring you closer to understanding your true purpose.

Finally, once you have a clearer sense of your "why," embrace it fully. Share it with others and let it guide your decisions. This newfound clarity can serve as a powerful motivator, helping you break free from the ordinary and pursue a life filled with passion and meaning. Remember, your journey is uniquely yours, and every step taken toward your purpose is a testament to your commitment to living an extraordinary life.

Embracing Change

Embracing change is a fundamental step toward unlocking your true potential. When you find yourself bored with the monotony of daily routines, it signifies a deeper yearning for growth and fulfillment. Change can be intimidating, but it is also an opportunity to discover new paths that lead to meaningful experiences. By shifting your mindset and viewing change as a chance for improvement, you can ignite the passion within you and propel yourself toward a more vibrant life.

To embrace change effectively, begin by identifying what aspects of your life feel stagnant. Acknowledging these feelings allows you to take proactive steps toward transformation. Whether it's changing your career, exploring new hobbies, or altering your daily habits, every small change adds up. It is crucial to cultivate a sense of curiosity about the world around you and to remain open to new experiences that can enrich your life.

As you embark on this journey of embracing change, remember that discomfort is often a sign of growth. The initial stages of change may bring uncertainty and fear, but these feelings are natural. Allow yourself to feel these emotions without letting them dictate your actions. Surround yourself with supportive individuals who encourage your growth and share their own experiences of change, as this can provide both inspiration and assurance.

The process of embracing change also requires you to set clear intentions. Determine what you want to achieve and visualize the outcome. This clarity will serve as a roadmap, guiding you as you navigate through challenges. Keep in mind that setbacks are part of the journey; they do not define your progress but rather contribute to your resilience and adaptability.

Ultimately, embracing change is about making a conscious decision to seek a more meaningful existence. By stepping out of your comfort zone and welcoming new possibilities, you ignite a spark that can lead to profound personal development. Remember, the journey is just as important as the destination, so celebrate your progress and remain committed to continuous growth as you break free from the ordinary.

Chapter 2: Shifting Your Mindset

Overcoming Limiting Beliefs

Overcoming limiting beliefs is a crucial step toward unlocking your true potential. These beliefs often stem from past experiences, societal conditioning, or negative self-talk, creating barriers that keep us from pursuing our dreams. To break free from the ordinary, it's essential to recognize these beliefs and challenge them head-on. This process begins with self-reflection, allowing you to identify the thoughts that hold you back, such as "I'm not good enough" or "I'll never succeed."

Once you've identified these beliefs, the next step is to reframe them. Instead of viewing setbacks as failures, consider them opportunities for growth. Adopting a growth mindset can be transformative; it shifts your perspective from one of limitation to one of possibility. As you practice this reframing, you'll start to see that your perceived obstacles can actually become stepping stones toward something greater.

Surrounding yourself with positive influences is another powerful strategy for overcoming limiting beliefs. Engage with individuals who inspire you, whether through books, podcasts, or conversations. Their stories of triumph can serve as motivation, reminding you that change is possible. Additionally, seek out communities that foster personal development; being part of a supportive network can reinforce your commitment to overcoming obstacles.

Visualization techniques can also play a vital role in overcoming limiting beliefs. By vividly imagining your desired outcomes, you create a mental image of success that can motivate you to take action. Picture yourself achieving your goals, experiencing the emotions associated with that success. This practice can help solidify your belief in your capabilities, pushing you to take the necessary steps toward meaningful change.

Finally, remember that overcoming limiting beliefs is a journey, not a destination. Celebrate your progress, no matter how small, and be patient with yourself. Growth takes time, and every step forward is a victory. Stay committed to your personal development, and you will find that the ordinary can become extraordinary, opening doors to a life filled with purpose and fulfillment.

Cultivating a Growth Mindset

Cultivating a growth mindset is essential for anyone looking to break free from the ordinary and embrace a life filled with meaning and purpose. It begins with recognizing that your abilities and intelligence can be developed through dedication and hard work. This perspective fosters resilience, encourages effort, and creates a love for learning, which is vital for personal development. By shifting your mindset, you open yourself up to new possibilities and experiences that can transform your daily routine.

One key aspect of nurturing a growth mindset is embracing challenges instead of avoiding them. When you face obstacles head-on, you learn valuable lessons that pave the way for future success. Each challenge you encounter is an opportunity for growth, as it pushes you out of your comfort zone and helps you discover your true potential. Instead of fearing failure, view it as a stepping stone toward achieving your goals and aspirations.

Another important factor is surrounding yourself with a supportive community. Engaging with like-minded individuals who share your desire for personal growth can significantly impact your journey. These connections provide encouragement, motivation, and constructive feedback that can help you stay focused on your path. Together, you can celebrate victories and learn from setbacks, reinforcing the belief that growth is a continuous process.

Moreover, practicing self-reflection and mindfulness can help you cultivate a growth mindset. Take time to assess your thoughts and feelings, and challenge any limiting beliefs that may hold you back. By being aware of your internal dialogue, you can replace negative thoughts with empowering affirmations that inspire action. This practice not only enhances your self-awareness but also strengthens your resolve to pursue meaningful change in your life.

Finally, remember that cultivating a growth mindset is a life-long journey. It requires patience, persistence, and a commitment to personal development. As you embrace this mindset, you'll find that each small step taken leads to greater fulfillment and a deeper sense of purpose. By igniting your potential and fostering a growth mindset, you can truly break free from the ordinary and create a life that resonates with your deepest desires and aspirations.

Chapter 3: Setting Meaningful Goals

～∽∽⌒

Defining Success on Your Terms

Success is a personal journey, unique to each individual. It is essential to define what success means to you, rather than allowing societal expectations or the opinions of others to dictate your path. Take a moment to reflect on what truly matters in your life. Consider your passions, values, and the legacy you wish to leave behind. When you embrace your definition of success, you empower yourself to pursue it wholeheartedly.

Many people feel stuck in their daily routines, yearning for something more meaningful. This stagnation often stems from a lack of clarity regarding personal goals. To ignite your potential, start by setting specific, achievable objectives that align with your vision of success. Break these goals down into manageable steps, and celebrate your progress along the way. Remember, each small victory brings you closer to your ultimate destination.

As you embark on this journey, it's important to cultivate a positive mindset. Surround yourself with supportive individuals who inspire you and share your aspirations. Engage in practices that boost your confidence, such as affirmations or visualizations.

By maintaining a focus on your goals and the reasons behind them, you will find the motivation to push through challenges and setbacks.

Moreover, be open to change and adaptable in your approach. The path to success is rarely linear, and obstacles may arise unexpectedly. Embrace these challenges as opportunities for growth and learning. Each experience, whether positive or negative, contributes to your understanding of yourself and your unique definition of success.

Ultimately, defining success on your terms is about living authentically and pursuing what brings you joy and fulfillment. It's about crafting a life that reflects your true self and aspirations. As you navigate your journey, stay committed to your vision, and remember that success is not just a destination but a continuous process of growth and self-discovery.

Creating an Actionable Plan

Creating an actionable plan is the cornerstone of transforming your aspirations into reality. It begins with identifying specific goals that resonate with your desire for personal growth and meaning. Instead of vague ambitions, break down your goals into clear, achievable tasks. This clarity not only fuels motivation but also provides a roadmap to follow, making the journey less daunting and more focused.

Next, prioritize your tasks based on urgency and importance. This step ensures that you dedicate your energy to what truly matters, preventing the overwhelm that often accompanies change. By tackling one task at a time, you build momentum and confidence, paving the way for further action. Remember, every small step taken is a victory that brings you closer to your larger vision.

As you move forward, it's crucial to set deadlines for your tasks. Deadlines create a sense of urgency and accountability, which can significantly enhance your productivity. They help you maintain focus and track your progress, allowing you to adjust your plan as necessary. Flexibility is key; if something isn't working, don't be afraid to reassess and alter your approach.

Additionally, seek support from those around you. Sharing your goals with friends, family, or mentors can provide encouragement and valuable insights. They can hold you accountable and offer different perspectives that may enhance your plan. Remember, you are not alone in this journey; collaboration can often lead to greater achievements than going solo.

Finally, celebrate your achievements, no matter how small. Recognizing your progress is vital for maintaining motivation and reinforcing your commitment to your goals. By acknowledging each step forward, you cultivate a positive mindset that fuels further action. Your journey toward a more meaningful life is not just about the destination, but also the growth you experience along the way.

Chapter 4: Building Resilience

The Power of Perseverance

Perseverance is the cornerstone of success and personal growth. It is the unwavering determination to keep pushing forward, even when the path is riddled with obstacles. For those feeling stuck in monotony, embracing perseverance can ignite a spark of motivation that transforms their daily routines into meaningful pursuits. By cultivating this mindset, individuals can break free from the ordinary and embark on journeys that resonate with their true aspirations.

When faced with challenges, it is easy to feel discouraged and contemplate giving up. However, true progress lies in the ability to rise after every fall. Each setback serves as a lesson, an opportunity to reassess goals and strategies. By viewing challenges as stepping stones rather than barriers, individuals can develop resilience. This shift in perspective fosters a sense of purpose and encourages the pursuit of passions that may have been previously overshadowed by routine.

The stories of those who have achieved remarkable feats often highlight their perseverance in the face of adversity. Icons in various fields have demonstrated that the road to success is rarely linear. They faced failures, criticism, and moments of doubt yet continued to strive toward their goals. These narratives serve as powerful reminders that perseverance is not just about enduring; it is about growing stronger with each challenge encountered along the way.

Engaging in personal development through perseverance also means setting realistic and meaningful goals. It requires patience and the understanding that significant change doesn't happen overnight. By breaking down larger aspirations into manageable steps, individuals can maintain motivation as they witness their progress. Celebrating small victories along the way reinforces the belief that they are capable of achieving great things, further fueling their desire to persevere.

Ultimately, the power of perseverance lies in its ability to transform ordinary lives into extraordinary journeys. It empowers individuals to step out of their comfort zones and pursue endeavors that resonate with their purpose. As they cultivate this vital trait, they unlock their potential and inspire those around them to do the same. The journey may be challenging, but the rewards of perseverance are immeasurable, leading to a life filled with meaning and fulfillment.

Learning from Failure

Failure is often viewed as a setback, but it can actually be one of the most powerful teachers in our lives. When we encounter failure, we are confronted with our limitations and the need to reassess our strategies. This process of reflection is crucial for personal growth. Rather than allowing failure to define us, we can choose to see it as an opportunity to learn and evolve. Embracing this mindset can transform our approach to challenges and inspire us to pursue our goals more passionately.

Each failure carries valuable lessons that can steer us in new directions. It forces us to analyze what went wrong and why, providing insights that success often does not. For instance, when we fail at a particular task, we gain a deeper understanding of our skills and the areas where we need improvement. This awareness is essential for anyone seeking to break free from monotony and find more meaningful pursuits in life. By dissecting our failures, we can identify patterns and develop strategies that align more closely with our true aspirations.

Moreover, many successful individuals attribute their achievements to their experiences with failure. Icons like J.K. Rowling and Thomas Edison faced numerous rejections and setbacks before reaching their goals. Their stories illustrate that resilience in the face of failure is a key ingredient for success. When we recognize that failure is a shared experience among high achievers, it can motivate us to persist through our own obstacles. This realization helps foster a culture of perseverance and a belief in our potential to achieve greatness.

The road to personal development is fraught with challenges, and learning from failure is a crucial part of that journey. It encourages us to step outside of our comfort zones and take risks. Every attempt, whether successful or not, adds to our experience and builds our confidence. By adopting a growth mindset, we can redefine our relationship with failure, viewing it as a stepping stone rather than a stumbling block.

In conclusion, learning from failure is not just about acknowledging mistakes; it is about using those experiences to fuel our personal development. As we advance in our lives, the lessons learned from our failures can guide us toward more fulfilling and meaningful pursuits. By embracing the insights gained from our setbacks, we empower ourselves to create a life that resonates with our true desires and aspirations. So, let us welcome failure as a mentor and move forward with renewed vigor and purpose.

Chapter 5: Breaking Free From Routine

❧

Identifying Your Comfort Zones

Identifying your comfort zones is the first step toward breaking free from the ordinary. Many individuals find themselves stuck in routines that may feel safe but offer little fulfillment. These comfort zones can be physical, emotional, or mental spaces where familiarity breeds complacency. Acknowledging these zones is crucial for anyone looking to advance and create a more meaningful life.

To begin this process, take a moment to reflect on your daily habits and routines. What activities do you engage in that feel comfortable but unchallenging? Perhaps you have a favorite coffee shop you visit every morning or a predictable work schedule that never varies. By pinpointing these comforting patterns, you can start to understand how they may be holding you back from exploring new opportunities.

Next, consider the emotions tied to your comfort zones. Are there particular feelings you associate with stepping outside your norm? Fear of failure, anxiety about the unknown, or even the simple dread of change can keep you anchored to familiar territory.

Recognizing these emotional barriers is essential, as it allows you to confront them head-on and understand their impact on your desire for growth.

Once you've identified these zones, challenge yourself to step outside of them, even if just slightly. This could mean trying a new hobby, meeting new people, or taking on a different project at work. Each small push against your comfort zone can build confidence and show you that discomfort can lead to growth and opportunity. Embrace the idea that stepping outside your comfort zone is not just a challenge, but a pathway to discovering what truly fulfills you.

Ultimately, identifying your comfort zones is about empowerment. It's about recognizing that while comfort can feel safe, it can also become a barrier to your potential. By acknowledging and challenging these zones, you open the door to a more dynamic and meaningful existence. Remember, every step you take toward discomfort is a step toward igniting your potential and reshaping your life.

Exploring New Opportunities

In a world that often feels monotonous, the quest for new opportunities can ignite the spark of inspiration within us. Many individuals find themselves trapped in a cycle of routine, longing for something more fulfilling. This chapter invites you to explore the vast landscape of possibilities that lie beyond your current situation. Embracing change and seeking new experiences can lead to personal growth and a renewed sense of purpose.

The first step in exploring new opportunities is recognizing the potential for change that exists in every moment. Whether it's a new hobby, a career shift, or simply altering your daily habits, each choice you make can open doors to exciting prospects. By stepping outside your comfort zone, you can discover hidden talents and passions that have been waiting to be unearthed. The journey of self-discovery begins when you dare to take that first leap into the unknown.

Networking and connecting with others can also play a crucial role in uncovering new opportunities. Engaging with people who share similar interests or who have ventured into different fields can provide valuable insights and inspiration. These connections can lead to collaborations that spark creativity and innovation, paving the way for unique paths you may not have considered before. Remember, every conversation is a chance to learn something new and expand your horizons.

Additionally, setting clear goals can guide your exploration of opportunities. By defining what you want to achieve, you create a roadmap that helps you measure progress and stay motivated. Goals serve as a constant reminder of your aspirations, ensuring that you remain focused on your journey toward a more meaningful existence. Celebrate small victories along the way, as they are stepping stones toward larger achievements.

Finally, maintaining a positive mindset is essential when exploring new opportunities. Challenges will arise, but viewing them as learning experiences rather than setbacks can transform your perspective. Embrace the idea that every experience, whether successful or not, contributes to your growth. As you navigate through your journey, remember that the pursuit of new opportunities is not just about changing your circumstances but about evolving into the best version of yourself.

Chapter 6: Harnessing Your Passion

Finding What Sets Your Soul on Fire

Finding what sets your soul on fire is an essential journey toward personal fulfillment. It's about identifying those passions and interests that resonate deeply within you, igniting a sense of purpose and enthusiasm. Many people find themselves stuck in a monotonous routine, feeling unfulfilled and yearning for something more significant. This chapter encourages you to explore the depths of your desires and dreams, paving the way for a more meaningful existence.

To begin this exploration, take a moment to reflect on what truly excites you. What activities make you lose track of time? What topics can you talk about for hours without feeling drained? By identifying these sparks of joy, you can start to piece together the puzzle of your passions. Remember, this journey is not merely about finding a career or hobby; it's about connecting with your authentic self and understanding what brings you genuine happiness.

Consider the moments in your life when you felt the most alive. Was it during a creative endeavor, a moment of connection with others, or perhaps an adventure in nature? These memories can serve as guiding lights, helping you navigate toward what truly sets your soul on fire. Embrace these experiences and learn from them; they are clues pointing you toward a more fulfilling path.

Additionally, don't shy away from trying new things. Sometimes, stepping outside your comfort zone can lead to unexpected discoveries. Attend workshops, join clubs, or volunteer for causes that resonate with you. Each new experience is a chance to uncover hidden interests and passions. The more you explore, the clearer your vision of what ignites your spirit will become.

Finally, be patient with yourself. Finding what sets your soul on fire is a journey, not a destination. It requires introspection, experimentation, and sometimes even trial and error. Allow yourself the grace to evolve and grow through this process. As you embark on this transformative journey, remember that the pursuit of passion is a deeply personal endeavor, and every step you take brings you closer to a more vibrant and meaningful life.

Turning Passion into Purpose

Many individuals find themselves trapped in a cycle of monotony, yearning for something more than the daily grind. This is where the journey of turning passion into purpose begins. Recognizing what ignites your enthusiasm is the first step toward transforming your life. It's essential to reflect on what activities make you lose track of time and fill you with joy, as these passions can guide you toward a more fulfilling existence.

Once you have identified your passions, the next step is to align them with your core values and beliefs. Passion alone is not enough; it must be rooted in a purpose that resonates with who you are at your core. Take the time to explore what truly matters to you and how your unique interests can serve a greater good. When you find the intersection of passion and purpose, you unlock the potential for a deeply meaningful life.

Setting goals is crucial in this transformative process. Goals provide a roadmap to turn your passion into actionable steps. Start small by setting achievable milestones that lead you closer to your ultimate vision. Celebrate each victory, no matter how minor, as these moments of progress fuel your motivation and reinforce your commitment to your purpose.

Embracing a growth mindset will help you navigate the challenges you may encounter along the way. Understand that setbacks are a natural part of any journey. Each obstacle presents an opportunity to learn and grow. By viewing challenges as stepping stones rather than barriers, you can maintain your momentum and continue moving toward your goals with determination and resilience.

Finally, surround yourself with a supportive community that shares your vision. Engaging with like-minded individuals can provide encouragement, inspiration, and accountability. Seek out mentors and peers who can offer guidance and share their own experiences. Together, you can foster an environment that nurtures your passion and purpose, making the journey not only fulfilling but also enriching.

Chapter 7: Surrounding Yourself with Positivity

The Impact of Your Environment

Your environment plays a crucial role in shaping your mindset and determining your potential. It encompasses everything from the people you surround yourself with to the physical spaces you inhabit. If you find yourself in a setting that stifles creativity or breeds negativity, it can be challenging to break free from the mundane. Conversely, a supportive and inspiring environment can ignite your passions and propel you toward meaningful change. Recognizing the importance of your surroundings is the first step toward transforming your life.

Imagine waking up every day in a space that energizes you, filled with colors, sounds, and people that uplift your spirit. This is not merely about aesthetics; it's about creating an atmosphere that fosters growth and innovation. Seek out environments that challenge you, whether that means joining a new community, attending workshops, or simply rearranging your workspace. By intentionally curating your surroundings, you open the door to new opportunities and perspectives that can dismantle the ordinary.

The people you interact with daily have a profound impact on your motivation and ambitions. Are you surrounded by those who inspire you, or do you find yourself in a circle that reinforces your fears and doubts? Surrounding yourself with positive influences can provide the encouragement you need to step outside your comfort zone. Engage with individuals who share your desire for growth, as their energy and aspirations can be contagious, leading to collaborative efforts that enhance your journey.

Additionally, consider the impact of your physical environment on your mental state. A cluttered, disorganized space can lead to feelings of overwhelm, while a clean, organized area can enhance focus and creativity. Make small changes, like decluttering your desk or adding plants to your workspace, to create a more inviting and stimulating atmosphere. These adjustments can help you cultivate a mindset that is more receptive to new ideas and opportunities.

Finally, remember that your environment is not fixed; it's malleable and can be reshaped according to your aspirations. Take proactive steps to alter your surroundings, whether through changes in your social circles or by seeking out new experiences that align with your goals. By consciously influencing your environment, you empower yourself to break free from the ordinary and embark on a journey of personal development that is rich with meaning and purpose.

Building a Supportive Network

Building a supportive network is crucial for anyone looking to break free from the ordinary and ignite their potential. Surrounding yourself with positive, driven individuals can create an environment that fosters growth and motivation. Each connection you make can open new doors, provide fresh perspectives, and inspire you to take bold steps toward your goals. Embrace the idea that your network can serve as a powerful catalyst for transformation in your life.

To start building this network, focus on finding individuals who share your aspirations and values. Attend workshops, seminars, or community events that align with your interests. Engage in conversations and actively seek out relationships with those who challenge and uplift you. Remember, the quality of your connections is more important than the quantity; a few supportive relationships can be more impactful than a large number of superficial ones.

Don't hesitate to reach out to mentors or role models who have successfully navigated paths similar to the one you aspire to take. Their experiences can provide invaluable insights and guidance, helping you avoid common pitfalls. A mentor can also serve as a source of accountability, encouraging you to stay committed to your journey of personal development and growth.

In addition to seeking out mentors, consider joining groups or organizations that align with your passions. Being part of a community not only provides support but also fosters a sense of belonging. Engaging with like-minded individuals can inspire creativity and collaboration, allowing you to explore different avenues and broaden your horizons in ways you might not have considered before.

Lastly, remember that building a supportive network is an ongoing process. As you evolve, so should your connections. Keep nurturing your relationships, and don't be afraid to reevaluate and expand your network as you grow. By actively engaging with others and fostering meaningful connections, you'll find that your journey toward a more meaningful life becomes not only achievable but also incredibly fulfilling.

Chapter 8: Taking Action

The Importance of Small Steps

In a world that often glorifies grand gestures and monumental changes, it's essential to remember the power of small steps. Each tiny action we take can lead to significant transformations over time. For those feeling stuck in a monotonous routine, embracing these small changes can breathe new life into their daily existence. Rather than waiting for a big, life-altering moment, focusing on incremental progress can create a sense of achievement and motivation.

Taking small steps allows for manageable adjustments that can lead to meaningful growth. Instead of overwhelming oneself with the idea of a complete overhaul, breaking goals into tiny, achievable tasks makes the journey less daunting. This method not only fosters a sense of accomplishment but also builds confidence over time. Each small victory adds up, creating a momentum that propels individuals toward their larger aspirations.

Moreover, small steps encourage consistency, which is crucial for personal development. When actions are broken down into bite-sized pieces, individuals are more likely to stick with them.

This consistency breeds habits that contribute to long-term success. Whether it's reading a few pages of a book daily or taking a short walk each morning, these habits can lead to significant changes in mindset and lifestyle.

Another advantage of small steps is the opportunity for reflection and adjustment. As one progresses through their journey, it's easier to evaluate what works and what doesn't when changes are incremental. This adaptability allows individuals to pivot as necessary, ensuring that their path remains aligned with their evolving goals and desires. Instead of feeling trapped by rigid plans, one can embrace fluidity and respond to their circumstances.

Ultimately, the importance of small steps lies in their ability to transform the ordinary into something extraordinary. For those yearning for meaning and fulfillment in their lives, these incremental changes can serve as stepping stones toward a richer existence. By focusing on small, consistent actions, individuals can cultivate a sense of purpose and direction, igniting their potential to break free from the mundane and embrace a more meaningful life.

Celebrating Progress

Celebrating progress is an essential part of personal development, as it fuels motivation and reinforces the commitment to pursuing meaningful changes. Every step taken toward your goals, no matter how small, deserves recognition. When we acknowledge our achievements, we create a positive feedback loop that encourages us to keep pushing forward and striving for more. This celebration can take many forms, from simply reflecting on your journey to sharing milestones with friends and family who support your growth.

One effective way to celebrate progress is by setting up a personal reward system. By aligning small rewards with your accomplishments, you create a sense of anticipation and excitement around achieving your goals. For instance, after completing a challenging task or reaching a specific milestone, treat yourself to something enjoyable, whether it's a favorite meal, a day out, or even a self-care activity. This not only makes the journey more enjoyable but also reinforces the notion that progress is worth celebrating.

Additionally, documenting your journey can serve as a powerful reminder of how far you've come. Keeping a journal or creating a visual representation of your goals and achievements allows you to look back at your progress with pride. This practice helps to maintain motivation, especially during times when you may feel stuck or discouraged. By revisiting past successes, you can reignite your passion for growth and remind yourself of the potential that lies within.

Sharing your progress with others can also amplify the joy of your accomplishments. By discussing your journey with friends, family, or a supportive community, you create an environment of encouragement and accountability. This social aspect of celebrating progress not only boosts your morale but also inspires those around you to pursue their own meaningful changes. Remember, your story can motivate others who may be feeling lost or unsure about their paths.

Finally, always take a moment to reflect on your journey and acknowledge the hard work you've put in. Celebrating progress isn't just about the end goal; it's about appreciating the growth and learning that occur along the way. Embrace the lessons learned, the challenges faced, and the strength gained. By doing so, you cultivate a mindset geared toward continuous improvement and fulfillment, allowing you to break free from the ordinary and truly ignite your potential.

Chapter 9: Embracing Lifelong Learning

The Benefits of Continuous Growth

Continuous growth is essential for anyone seeking to advance beyond the ordinary. It offers the opportunity to break free from the monotony of daily routines and explore new avenues of personal development. Engaging in continuous growth allows individuals to challenge themselves, fostering resilience and adaptability. This journey not only enhances self-awareness but also cultivates a sense of purpose that is often missing in repetitive lifestyles.

One of the most significant benefits of continuous growth is the boost it provides to motivation. When individuals set new goals and pursue new skills, they ignite a passion for learning that can transform their outlook on life. This intrinsic motivation propels them forward, encouraging them to take risks and embrace change with enthusiasm. In this way, growth becomes a catalyst for a more vibrant and fulfilling life.

Moreover, continuous growth enhances one's ability to overcome obstacles. As people push their boundaries, they develop a toolkit of strategies and mindsets that enable them to face challenges head-on. This resilience is invaluable, as it not only prepares individuals for future difficulties but also instills a deep confidence in their capabilities. With each step taken outside their comfort zones, they reinforce the belief that they can achieve meaningful change.

In addition to personal benefits, a commitment to continuous growth positively impacts relationships. As individuals evolve, they bring fresh perspectives and ideas to their interactions with others. This openness fosters deeper connections and encourages collaboration, which can lead to new opportunities in both personal and professional realms. The ripple effect of one person's growth can inspire those around them to embark on their own journeys of development.

Ultimately, embracing continuous growth is about creating a more meaningful life. It encourages individuals to seek out experiences that align with their values and aspirations, rather than settling for the status quo. By prioritizing personal development, they not only enrich their own lives but also contribute to the collective growth of their communities. With each step taken toward growth, individuals move closer to realizing their full potential, transforming the ordinary into the extraordinary.

Seeking New Experiences

In a world that often feels monotonous, seeking new experiences can be the key to unlocking your true potential. Many individuals find themselves trapped in a cycle of routine, where days blend into one another without distinction. This mundane existence can lead to feelings of dissatisfaction and a yearning for something more meaningful. By actively pursuing new experiences, you can break free from the ordinary and reignite your passion for life.

Exploring new activities, whether they be hobbies, travel, or learning opportunities, can provide fresh perspectives that enrich your life. Each new experience acts as a stepping stone toward personal growth, challenging you to step outside your comfort zone. The thrill of trying something unfamiliar can spark creativity and motivation, igniting a desire to continue seeking out adventures. Embrace the unknown, for it is often in these moments that we discover our true selves.

Additionally, seeking new experiences fosters resilience and adaptability. Life is full of surprises, and the ability to navigate change is crucial for personal development. When you expose yourself to different situations, you build confidence and learn to embrace uncertainty. This ability to adapt not only enhances your personal growth but also equips you with valuable skills that can be applied in various aspects of life, including career advancement.

Moreover, engaging with new experiences allows you to connect with others who share similar interests. Building a network of like-minded individuals can lead to meaningful relationships and collaborations. These connections often provide support and encouragement, further motivating you to pursue your goals. The shared journey of exploration can be incredibly rewarding, as you learn from others while also contributing your own insights and experiences.

In conclusion, seeking new experiences is essential for anyone looking to break free from the mundane and ignite their potential. The journey of personal development is enriched by the willingness to embrace change and explore the unfamiliar. By stepping out of your comfort zone, you open the door to a world filled with opportunities for growth, connection, and fulfillment. Remember, every new experience is a chance to learn, grow, and ultimately, transform your life.

Chapter 10: Living a Meaningful Life

Aligning Actions with Values

Aligning your actions with your values is a vital step toward achieving a fulfilling life. When you understand what truly matters to you, you can begin to make decisions that resonate with your core beliefs. This alignment not only fosters a sense of purpose but also ignites a passion that drives you to pursue your goals relentlessly. Whether it's personal growth, career changes, or new adventures, living in accordance with your values transforms mundane routines into meaningful journeys.

To start aligning your actions with your values, take time for self-reflection. Identify what you genuinely value in life—be it family, health, creativity, or contribution to society. Write these values down and assess how your current lifestyle reflects them. Are there areas where your actions contradict these values? Recognizing these discrepancies is the first step in making the necessary adjustments that lead to a more authentic existence.

Next, set specific goals that embody your values. For instance, if one of your core values is helping others, you might consider volunteering or pursuing a career in social work. Setting goals that align with your values provides clarity and direction, ensuring that your efforts are not just productive but also meaningful. This alignment fuels motivation and helps you break free from the ordinary, paving the way for a more vibrant and engaged life.

As you commit to aligning your actions with your values, embrace the journey of transformation, even when it's challenging. Change is often uncomfortable, but it is necessary for growth. Surround yourself with supportive individuals who encourage you to stay true to your values. Their support can be a powerful motivator, helping you to overcome obstacles and keep moving forward on your path to fulfillment.

Ultimately, aligning your actions with your values is about creating a life that resonates with your true self. This alignment not only enhances your sense of purpose but also inspires others around you. As you break free from the mundane and pursue a life of meaning, you become a beacon of motivation for those who seek to ignite their potential. Remember, every small step you take toward alignment is a step toward a more extraordinary life.

Making a Difference in the World

Making a difference in the world begins with recognizing that every small action counts. Many individuals feel overwhelmed by the scale of issues facing society today, but it's essential to understand that change starts with you. By taking even the smallest steps toward positive action, you can contribute to a larger movement that inspires others and creates a ripple effect of goodwill. This realization can ignite a passion within you, pushing you to break free from the monotony of daily life and pursue a more meaningful existence.

Identifying your unique strengths and interests is crucial in this journey. Reflect on what excites you and where your talents lie. Whether it's volunteering, advocating for a cause, or initiating a community project, your skills can be utilized to make a significant impact. Engaging in activities that align with your passions will not only fulfill you but also motivate others to join your mission, fostering a sense of community and shared purpose.

As you embark on this quest to make a difference, surround yourself with like-minded individuals. Building a network of motivated people can enhance your efforts and provide support during challenging times. Share your goals and collaborate on projects that resonate with your mutual interests. This collective energy can amplify your impact, creating a powerful force for change that extends beyond individual efforts.

Embrace the idea that every effort, no matter how small, contributes to the greater good. Celebrate the victories, both big and small, and learn from the setbacks. Each experience will shape your journey and refine your approach, making you more effective in your endeavors. Remember, making a difference is not just about the end result; it's about the growth and transformation you experience along the way.

Finally, remain committed to your purpose and stay open to new opportunities. The world is constantly changing, and as you grow, so too will your ability to impact it positively. Keep seeking ways to inspire others and lead by example. Your dedication to making a difference can motivate those around you to step out of their comfort zones and pursue their own paths of meaningful change. Together, we can create a brighter future for ourselves and for generations to come.

Chapter 11: Reflecting and Reassessing

~~~

The Power of Reflection

In the hustle and bustle of our daily lives, we often overlook the immense power of reflection. Taking a moment to pause and evaluate our experiences allows us to gain insights that can lead to significant changes. Reflection is not merely about thinking; it's about understanding our actions, motivations, and the paths we take. By engaging in this practice, we can uncover patterns that may be holding us back from advancing toward our true potential.

One of the greatest benefits of reflection is the clarity it brings. When we step back and analyze our choices, we can identify what truly matters to us. This process helps us distinguish between activities that are merely time-fillers and those that bring genuine fulfillment. By recognizing our core values and passions, we can make more informed decisions that align with our desire for a meaningful life.

Moreover, reflection fosters personal growth by encouraging us to learn from our past experiences. Every success and failure carries lessons that can propel us forward. By reflecting on what we've encountered, we can develop resilience and adaptability. This growth mindset equips us to embrace challenges with confidence, knowing that each experience contributes to our journey of self-improvement.

Another important aspect of reflection is its role in cultivating gratitude. When we take time to contemplate our experiences, we often find moments of joy and learning that we might have missed in the rush of daily life. This gratitude not only enhances our overall well-being but also fuels our motivation to pursue new opportunities. It reminds us that even the mundane can hold meaning if we choose to see it.

Finally, incorporating reflection into our routine can act as a catalyst for change. It empowers us to break free from the ordinary by igniting our passions and ambitions. As we reflect on our desires for a more fulfilling life, we become more attuned to the possibilities around us. By making reflection a regular practice, we can continuously realign ourselves with our goals and aspirations, creating a life that is not just lived but truly experienced.

Adjusting Your Course

Adjusting your course is a vital step in the journey to personal growth and fulfillment. Many individuals find themselves stuck in the monotony of their daily routines, feeling a sense of boredom and dissatisfaction. This often signals a need for change, and recognizing this is the first step toward igniting your potential. Embrace the discomfort that comes with stagnation; it can be a powerful motivator to seek out new paths and experiences.

To effectively adjust your course, it is important to reflect on your current situation and identify what aspects of your life are unfulfilling. Take the time to evaluate your daily activities, relationships, and career choices. Ask yourself what truly brings you joy and meaning. This process of introspection will help you clarify your desires and set the foundation for meaningful change. Remember, the journey toward a more fulfilling life often begins with self-awareness.

Once you have a clearer understanding of what you want, it's time to set actionable goals. These goals should be specific, measurable, and aligned with your newfound insights. Consider breaking them down into smaller, manageable steps to prevent feeling overwhelmed. Creating a roadmap for your journey will not only keep you motivated but also provide a sense of direction as you strive for a life that resonates with your core values.

As you embark on this journey of adjustment, be prepared to face challenges and setbacks. Change can be daunting, but it is also an opportunity for growth. Surround yourself with supportive individuals who encourage your pursuits and share your aspirations. Engaging with a community of like-minded individuals can provide not only motivation but also valuable insights and encouragement as you navigate your new path.

Finally, remember that adjusting your course is not a one-time event but an ongoing process. Life is dynamic, and as you grow, your goals and desires may evolve. Stay flexible and open to new opportunities, and regularly reassess your path. This commitment to continuous growth will not only help you break free from the ordinary but will also lead to a richer, more meaningful life.

Chapter 12: Sustaining Your Momentum

❧

Creating Lasting Habits

Creating lasting habits is essential for anyone looking to break free from the ordinary and ignite their potential. It begins with understanding that change is not a one-time event but a continuous journey. To cultivate meaningful habits, one must first identify the areas of life that feel stagnant or unfulfilling. This self-reflection lays the groundwork for purposeful transformation, allowing individuals to focus on what truly matters to them.

Once you have pinpointed the aspects of your life that require change, the next step is to set clear and achievable goals. These goals act as a roadmap, guiding you through the process of habit formation. It's crucial to start small; rather than trying to overhaul your entire routine at once, focus on integrating one new habit at a time. This incremental approach makes the transition more manageable and increases the likelihood of success.

Accountability plays a vital role in creating lasting habits. Whether it's through a friend, mentor, or a support group, sharing your goals with others can provide the encouragement needed to stay on track. When you know someone is cheering you on, it becomes easier to push through challenges and setbacks. Celebrate your progress, no matter how small, as this reinforces your commitment and fosters a positive mindset.

Incorporating habits into your daily routine requires consistency and patience. Establishing a specific time and place for your new habits can significantly enhance your ability to maintain them. Over time, these repeated actions will become second nature, allowing you to effortlessly integrate them into your life. Remember, perseverance is key; even when motivation wanes, the discipline of sticking to your new habits will keep you moving forward.

Ultimately, creating lasting habits is about aligning your actions with your values and aspirations. As you continuously refine your habits, you will find yourself not only advancing in your personal development journey but also experiencing a profound sense of fulfillment. Embrace the process, remain committed, and watch as your life transforms into something truly meaningful and extraordinary.

Staying Motivated in the Long Run

Staying motivated in the long run can be a challenge, especially for those who feel stuck in their daily routines. The key is to ignite your passion by setting clear and meaningful goals. When you have a vision of what you want to achieve, it becomes easier to push through the obstacles that may arise. A well-defined goal acts as a beacon, guiding you toward the life you desire. Remember, motivation is not just a fleeting feeling; it is a commitment to your growth and development.

To maintain motivation, it is essential to celebrate small victories along the way. Acknowledging these milestones can reinvigorate your spirit and remind you of your progress. Whether it's completing a project, learning a new skill, or simply sticking to your routine, take the time to reflect on your achievements. This practice not only boosts your confidence but also reinforces your dedication to your long-term goals. Celebrate your journey, for every step counts.

Another effective strategy for staying motivated is to surround yourself with positive influences. Engage with individuals who inspire and uplift you. This network of like-minded people can provide encouragement and accountability, making it easier to stay on track. Share your aspirations with them, and they will help you navigate the challenges you may face. Their support can act as an essential catalyst in your pursuit of something more meaningful.

Incorporating variety into your routine can also help sustain your motivation. When monotony sets in, it can be easy to lose sight of your objectives. By introducing new activities, challenges, or learning opportunities, you can keep your mind engaged and excited. Explore different hobbies, take courses, or volunteer in your community. Each new experience enriches your life and reinforces your commitment to personal growth.

Lastly, always remind yourself of the bigger picture. Reflect on why you embarked on this journey in the first place. Your purpose will serve as a powerful motivator during tough times. Write down your reasons, and revisit them when your motivation wanes. Staying connected to your "why" will not only keep you focused but will also empower you to overcome any hurdles in your path. Remember, the journey to a more meaningful life is a marathon, not a sprint, and every effort you invest will bring you closer to your true potential.

About the Author

George Hatcher is a man who has always believed that the world is full of opportunities waiting for those bold enough to seize them. With a ninth-grade education and a wealth of unique experiences, he has faced the ups and downs of life head-on. At the age of 20, while serving time, George took the initiative to complete the assignments and tests necessary to earn his high school diploma. His own life is a treasure trove of stories waiting to be uncovered.

Over the years, George has enjoyed a diverse career as an entrepreneur, consultant, and strategist. He has served as a peacemaker for athletes and their parents, as well as a crisis management advisor for physicians and attorneys, achieving considerable success in client development and public relations. He is a licensed boxing manager in California, though he currently has no boxers signed.

George has logged over 200,000 air miles annually through business travel and pleasure trips with his wife. However, since the onset of COVID-19 in 2020, his travel has come to a halt. Now, in retirement, George finds that life remains an ongoing adventure. Unfortunately, he is fighting several new battles that he never anticipated, yet he continues to discover something new with each step.

As a passionate storyteller, George has published a dozen books and finds immense joy in writing. With the world opening up again, he has seized the opportunity to immerse himself fully in his literary pursuits. He currently resides in Rancho Mirage, California, with his wife, Molly, his partner for 60 years, and their home is filled with three cats and one macaw named Peaches. Each experience in his life has taught him invaluable lessons about adaptability, perseverance, and a touch of luck. Like the person who hits their head just to feel the pleasure of stopping, George has made his share of mistakes—some more than once. He hopes others can learn from them as he has.

Now devoted entirely to writing, George Hatcher invites others to join him on this remarkable journey, filled with lessons and stories that showcase the beauty of life's unpredictability.

A longer bio is on his website at
http://georgehatcher.com/bio/bio.html

www.ingramcontent.com/pod-product-compliance
Lightning Source LLC
Chambersburg PA
CBHW071351130626
46556CB00005B/2135